THE SAYINGS OF
MRS. SOLOMON

Being the Confessions of the
Seven Hundredth Wife as Revealed to

Helen Rowland

Published by Greenleaf Press
Lebanon, Tennessee

Internet: www.greenleafpress.com
3761 Highway 109 N., Unit D
Lebanon, TN 37087
615-449-1617

GREENLEAF
P · R · E · S · S

TABLE OF CONTENTS

And Verily, a Woman Need Know But One Man Well, in Order to Understand *ALL* Men; Whereas a Man May Know All Women and Understand Not One of Them.

GREETING

Hearken, my daughter, and give ear unto my wisdom, that thou mayest understand man – his goings and his comings, his stayings out and his return in the morning, his words of honey and his ways of guile.

Beloved, question me not, whence I have learned of man, his secrets. Have I not known one man well? And verily, a woman need know but one man, in order to understand *all* men; whereas a man may know all women and understand not one of them.

For men are of but one pattern, whereof thou needest but to discover the secret combination; but women are as the *Yale* lock – no two of them are alike.

Lo! What a paradox is man – even a puzzle which worketh backward!

He mistaketh a sweet scent for a sweet disposition, and a subtile sachet for a subtile mind.

He voweth, "I admire a discreet woman!" – and inviteth the froward blonde of the chorus to supper.

[7]

GREETING

He muttereth unto his wife, "Lo! I will go unto the corner for a cigar" – and behold, he wandereth unto many corners and returneth by a circular route.

He kisseth the woman whom he loveth not, and avoideth her whom he loveth, lest his heart become entangled. Yea, he seeketh always the wrong woman that he may forget his heart's desire.

Yet, whichever he weddeth, he regretteth it all the days of his life.

SELAH.

For a Lone Woman in a Great Restaurant Looketh Pitiful; But an Husband Looketh Like a Real *Tip*.

BOOK OF HUSBANDS

Chapter One

Verily my Daughter, an husband is a Good Thing. He giveth the house a "finished" look, even as a rubber plant and a door-plate.

He suggesteth ready-money, and is an *adornment* like unto a potted palm upon the piazza.

When he sitteth beside thee in the tabernacle, he is as a certificate of respectability; yea in the eyes of society, he is better than a written recommendation.

Verily, he is as necessary unto thy dinner table as a centerpiece, and more impressive than cut flowers and a butler in livery.

When he taketh thee abroad to dine, the waiter shall not lead thee into dim and draughty corners, but shall run nimbly and place thee in a choice spot within *hearing* of the music.

For a lone woman in a great restaurant looketh pitiful but an husband looketh like a real *tip*.

When thou goest unto an hotel in his company, the clerk shall not offer thee a room upon the air-shaft; and the bell-boys shall answer thy ring with flying feet and a glad smile. For an husband is as good as much credit.

Yea, when thou goest forth to shop, saying "Send this thing to *Mrs*. Jones," the clerk shall treat thee *almost* as an equal.

Women shall not gossip about thee, and men shall come unto thy teas with an easy mind, knowing thou canst have no designs upon them. Thy family shall call thee "*settled,*" and no woman shall call thee "Poor Thing!"

Therefore, I say unto thee, if thou findest thine husband less than thine ideal, weep not, but be of good cheer.

For what profiteth it a woman, though she have every other luxury in all the world, and have not a *little husband* in her home?

[14]

BOOK OF HUSBANDS

Chapter Two

A PERFECT husband, who can find one? For his price is far above gold bonds. The heart of his wife rejoiceth in him, and he shall have no lack of encouragement.

He worketh willingly with his hands and bringeth home *all* his shekels.

He riseth without calling and lifteth the ice from off the dumbwaiter. He starteth the kitchen range. He considereth his wife, and kisseth her *occasionally.*

Six days of the week doth he labor for his moneys, and upon the seventh doeth chores within the house for *relaxation.*

With his own hands he runneth the lawn mower and washeth the dog.

He layeth his hands to the parlor curtains and putteth up the portieres.

He hooketh up his wife's dresses up the back, *without* mutterings.

[15]

BOOK OF HUSBANDS

He putteth the cat out by night.

He is *not* afraid of the cook.

His ashes fall not upon the carpet, and his cigarette burneth not holes in the draperies.

For he doeth his smoking on the piazza.

He weareth everlasting socks and seweth on his own buttons.

His overcoat doeth him two seasons.

Yet, when he ventureth abroad with his wife he donneth a *dress suit* without grumbling.

The grouch knoweth him not and his breakfast always pleaseth him. His mouth is filled with praises for his wife's cooking. He doth *not* expect chicken salad from left-over veal, neither the making of lobster patties from an ham-bone.

His wife is known within the gates, when she sitteth among the officers of her Club, by the fit of her gowns and her imported hats. He luncheth meagrely upon a sandwich that he may adorn her with fine jewels. He grumbleth not at the bills.

[16]

BOOK OF HUSBANDS

He openeth his mouth with praises and *noteth* her new frock. And the word of flattery is on his tongue.

He perceiveth not the existence of *other* women.

He may be *trusted* to mail a letter.

Lo, many men have I met in the world, but none like unto *him*.

Yet have ye all seen him — in your *dreams!*

BOOK OF HUSBANDS

Chapter Three

BEHOLD, my Daughter, the Lord maketh a man – but the *wife* maketh an *husband*. For Man is but the raw material whereon a woman putteth the *finishing touches*.

Yea, and whatsoever pattern of husband thou selectest, thou shalt find him like unto a shop-made garment, which must be trimmed over and cut down, and ironed out, and built up to fit the matrimonial situation.

Verily, the best of husbands hath many raw edges, and many unnecessary pleats in his temper, and many wrinkles in his disposition, which must be removed.

Lo, I charge thee, be wary in thy choice. For, many shall call, but few shall propose. And, a wise damsel shall with difficulty select that which fitteth her disposition and matcheth her tastes — even that which shall not pinch upon the bank account, neither stretch upon the truth, neither shrink nor run nor fade.

BOOK OF HUSBANDS

At the second-hand counter thou shalt find many widowers, which have been remodelled by another hand. And these are easy to acquire. Yet an hand-me-down may have been spoiled in the making, and become frayed at the edges of the temper, and shiny on the seamy-side.

But a *bachelor* who hath passed forty is a *remnant*; and there is no good material left in him. His sentiments are moth-eaten and his tender speeches shopworn. His manners shall require much basting and his morals many patches. The gloss hath been rubbed off his illusions and the color hath gone out of his emotions. Yet, a clever damsel shall, peradventure, take one of these and remodel him to seem as new.

For the happiest wife is not she that getteth the best husband, but she that maketh the best of that which she getteth. Verily, verily, an husband is a *work of art* which must be executed by hand; for there is no factory which turneth them out to order.

[19]

BOOK OF HUSBANDS

Chapter Four

GO to the *lemon grove*, oh, thou Scholarette! For no woman with *brains* hath ever plucked a peach in the Garden of Matrimony.

Nay, it is not given unto one woman to possess both real ability and a real husband.

For unto a successful woman an husband is but an adjunct; and no man yearneth to be an *annex!*

Alas! He preferreth soft, sweet things, and unto him a woman that knoweth her own mind is an abomination.

Verily, verily, a woman with *nerves* affecteth a man as a mosquito that buzzeth throughout a summer night. She wearieth him.

But a woman with *nerve* is as a cold bath on a winter morning. She shocketh him!

Lo, an intelligent *opinion* in the mouth of a woman horrifieth a man even as the scissors in the mouth of a babe.

BOOK OF HUSBANDS

And a wife with *judgment* which exceedeth his own is more uncanny than a pet parrot which saith the appropriate thing at the right moment. She appalleth him!

My Daughter, in all the land dost thou know of one clever woman who hath been happily married?

Nay! For I say unto thee there can be but one mind, one opinion, and one *throne* in an household; and every man claimeth these for himself.

Then, oh, thou Temperamental One, whatsoever thou receivest in the *love game*, accept it gladly and rejoice thereat.

For, whether it be a babe torn from the cradle or an octogenarian spared from the grave; whether it be a left-over bachelor, or an hand-me-down widower; though thou weddest fourscore times, thou shalt do *no better!*

Verily, verily, in the life of every woman, there cometh a season when she yearneth for *sentiment*, and neither the love of her "art" nor the adoration of a poodle dog is sufficient.

[21]

BOOK OF HUSBANDS

And a little unhappiness *with* an husband is more to be desired than great loneliness *without* one.

Go to! Life without one of these is as spaghetti without sauce and more insipid than bouillon without salt.

Therefore, my Daughter, gather in the Lemon which Fate awardeth thee and let thine heart be comforted.

For though wine is desirable, yet lemonade is not to be despised; and even an Highbrow shall find an husband an agreeable distraction from *serious* things!

BOOK OF HUSBANDS

Chapter Five

HOW long, oh thou Credulous One, wilt thou continue to marry for a *change*; and the lawyers delight in their fees, and the neighbors in their "I-said-so's"?

For lo, though there be many varieties of men, there is but *one* kind of husband!

Yea, though a man wed seven times seven times, he maketh not the *same* mistake twice.

But the woman who weddeth a second time, *repeateth* her own history.

Verily, verily, if thou wilt but close thine eyes, thou canst not perceive from his words, neither from the cloves upon his breath, nor the ardor of his greeting, whether it be thy *first* or thy *second* husband, that kisseth thee.

For one man's chin is as rough as another's, and one man's lies are as smooth as another's.

One man's razor is as sacred as another's, and one man's excuses are as old as another's.

[23]

BOOK OF HUSBANDS

One man roareth, like unto another, when he is hungry.

One man growleth, like unto another, when he is fed.

One man groaneth, like unto another, when he hath over-eaten.

One man looketh as uncanny as another without a collar, and as weird as another without a shave.

One man streweth his cigar ashes upon the carpet, and leaveth his stubs in the pin-tray, even as another.

One man burieth himself in the pillows in the morning, and in the newspapers in the evening, and refuseth to be torn therefrom – even as another.

One man offereth up the morning and evening growl, and celebrateth the Sunday forenoon grouch as regularly as another.

Why, then, wilt thou continue to hearken unto their promises ? For, before marriage, *all* men are *promising*; but matrimony is a chemical which transmuteth each and every one of them from a lover

[24]

into a critic, from an admirer into a scoffer, from an adorer into a judge, and from a slave into a sultan.

Verily, verily, there is this difference only in husbands:

That the first maketh thee weep;

The second maketh thee wonder;

But the third maketh thee weary!

SELAH.

Bring the Cushion for His Head, and the Footstool for His Feet, and Feed Him from the Chafing-dish with the Fruits of Thine Own Cooking.

BOOK OF FLIRTS

Chapter One

L O! wondrous are the workings of a man's heart, my Daughter.

His love is a thing which riseth and falleth as the stock market; yea, like a football that goeth up, it descendeth swiftly.

Behold, when a man first meeteth a damsel, she pleaseth his eyes. Moreover, she is different from the girl *before* and affordeth a pleasant change. He adoreth her from afar and indulgeth in foolish pipedreams. He investeth in new cravats and is particular concerning his collars.

He calleth at first, timidly; he getteth on the good side of the family. He bringeth burnt offerings of expensive flowers and sweets from Huyler's. He readeth the Rubaiyat unto her and inviteth her to meet his *sister*.

And, behold, there cometh a day when he kisseth her suddenly and without warning.

And another when he kisseth her again – easily.

And another when he kisseth her much and often.

[29]

And another when he kisseth her more casually.

And another when he departeth early, and kisseth her but once – "Good night".

And another when he *faileth* to call.

Then, peradventure, she writeth him a letter – which he putteth in his pocket and forgetteth to answer. She summoneth him over the telephone and he goeth into the booth wearily. She reproacheth and revileth him. He picketh a quarrel.

She sobbeth "All is over between us!" He answereth "Oh, very well! Even as thou sayest!"

And, in time, he meeteth another damsel and doeth it *all over again*. Yea, the selfsame programme he repeateth unto the letter; yet, he *never* tireth.

For lo! though a man hath eaten his fill at one meal, why shall he lack appetite for the next?

Then, I charge thee, my Daughter, when love beginneth, question not any man how it will end; for it is only in the *beginning* of things that a man is interested; even in the cream from off the jug, the

[30]

bubble of the champagne, the meat on the peach, and – the *first kiss* of a woman.

Yet, what mattereth the end? Is not the end of the cream, skimmed milk; and the end of a cigar, a stub; and the end of a peach, a stone; and the end of champagne, dregs; and the end of love, a quarrel? And which of these would ye choose?

Verily, the flirtations of a man s bachelor days are, in passing, as the courses of the love-feast; but a *wife* is the black coffee which *settleth* him.

BOOK OF FLIRTS

Chapter Two

MARVELLOUS, oh, my Daughter, is the way of a man with women; for every man hath a *method* and each his favorite *stunt*. And the stunt that he hath found to work successfully with one damsel shall be practised upon each in turn, even unto the finest details thereof.

Behold, one man shall come unto thee saying:

"How foolish are the sentimentalists! But, as for *me*, my motives are altruistic and disinterested; and a woman's *friendship* is what I most desire." Yet, I charge thee, seek among his women "friends" and thou shalt not find an *homely* damsel in all their number.

For this is the *platonic* stunt.

Now, another shall try thee by a simpler method.

Lo, suddenly and without warning, he shall arise and catch thee in his arms. And when thou smitest him upon the cheek, he shall be overcome with humiliation, crying:

"I could not *help* it!"

[32]

BOOK OF FLIRTS

Yet be not persuaded, but put him *down* without mercy, lest peradventure, he kiss thee again.

For this is the *impetuous* stunt.

Yet observe how still another seeketh to be more subtile.

Mark how he sitteth afar off and talketh of love in the *abstract*; how he calleth three times a week, yet remaineth always *impersonal*; how he praiseth the shape of thine hand and admireth thy rings, yet toucheth not so much as the *tips* of thy fingers.

"Lo," he thinketh in his heart, "I shall keep her guessing. Yea, I shall wrack her soul with thoughts of how I may be brought to subjection. And when she can no longer contain her curiosity, then will she seek to *lure* me, and I shall gather her in mine arms."

And this is the *elusive* stunt.

But, I say unto thee, my Daughter, each of these is but as a chainstitch unto a rose pattern, beside him that playeth the *frankly devoted*.

BOOK OF FLIRTS

For all women are unto him as one woman – and that one *putty*.

Lo, the look of "adoration" in his eyes is like unto the curl in his hair, *always* there ; and he weareth his "protecting manner" as naturally and as constantly as his linen collar.

He is so attentive and the *thoughtful thing* cometh unto him as second nature.

Yea, though there be twenty damsels in the room, yet shall each be made to think in her heart : "Lo, I am *it!*"

Verily, verily, all the days of his life he shall be waited on and cooed over and coddled by women; and his way shall be as one continuous path of conquests and thornless roses.

For this is the Stunt of *Stunts*!

[34]

BOOK OF FLIRTS

Chapter Three

I CHARGE thee, my Daughter, seek not to break a man's heart; for it is like unto family pride, or a pin, which may be *bent*, but *cannot* be broken! Yea, it is as a ball of India rubber which reboundeth easily after the worst shocks.

Lo, the heart of a woman is full of soft spots in which every man she hath once loved occupieth a "cozy corner". She lingereth tenderly over the grave of a dead love; but a man flingeth a spadeful of earth thereon and proceedeth to dig a *new* one. And his heart is as a great cemetery!

A woman keepeth a bundle of love-letters tied in faded ribbons; but a man cleaneth his pipe bowl cheerfully with the stem of the rose which the *girl-before-the-last* hath worn in her hair.

A woman remembereth the dress she hath worn and the song she hath sung for each particular man; but a man remembereth not the scent of violet sachet when the odor of heliotrope is in his nostrils.

And, after *six* months, when he cometh by chance upon an old glove or a lock of hair at the bottom of

[35]

his trunk, he casteth it into the fire, muttering, "Now, who the devil put *that* thing there?"

A woman recollecteth each pet name by which she hath been called; she alloweth no *two* men to label her alike. But unto a man, *every* woman becometh in turn "Little Girl" or "Baby" or "Honey."

Lo, he is as one that playeth with skulls and sporteth with the bones of his ancestors; for he holdeth nothing sacred.

He eraseth one face from the tablet of memory, and draweth another across it.

He changeth his object of thought as readily as he changeth his clothes and his political opinions.

For a woman's love is a slow flame which smouldereth always, but a man's love is like unto a skyrocket, which sputtereth out and cannot be rekindled.

Verily, his "past" is always *quite* past, and his dead loves are quite dead. And there is *nothing* which is more wearisome unto him than the memory of yesterday's wine, or yesterday's flirtation.

BOOK OF FLIRTS

Chapter Four

MY Daughter, there are many styles of kisses, and they come in endless patterns, even as Oriental rugs.

There is the kiss that sootheth and the kiss that thrilleth, the kiss that nattereth and the kiss that is a pastime. But the best of all kisses is the *first* kiss; for it is the most difficult.

Yet, in all the days of thy life, no two men shall kiss thee *alike*. For one man shall regard thy kisses as a boon, and another shall regard them as an amusement; but an husband shall consider them, as the shaving of his chin, a morning duty.

Hast thou scorned a man's kisses?

Then will he exalt thee, saying "Lo! she is *very* proper." For he can think of no other reason why thou shouldst not desire to kiss him.

Yet if thou hast consented to kiss only *one* man, he will say unto himself, "Verily, it is her habit. So doeth she with *all* mankind." For every man judgeth thee by the way in which thou treatest *him*.

BOOK OF FLIRTS

If a man kisseth thy hand gracefully, beware of him; for this is the habit of an accomplished flirt, which hath been acquired by much practice.

But if he kisseth thee first upon the forehead, and then upon the eyelids, and then upon the lips, thou mayest choose thy wedding gown and decide upon thy bridesmaids.

Lo, kissing is a fine art, and there are many artists; and one shall take a kiss from thee as though he doeth thee a favor, and another shall take a kiss as though he had taken thy pocketbook.

Yet, no man shall ever understand why thou seemest pleased, or why thou waxest wroth, when he kisseth thee; for it is all in the way of his wooing.

Verily, verily, a man who kisseth a woman with his *hat* on shall be annihilated.

But he, that kisseth her as though he had *never* kissed *before* and never should kiss *again*, shall wear an halo in her sight. For he knoweth the Art of *Arts*.

BOOK OF FLIRTS

Chapter Five

L O, my Daughter, a man came unto me saying: "Let me be thy slave. For, behold, I am *all devotion*. And it is my delight to serve a fair woman."

And I looked at him and smiled sadly.

For I knew that he was *invulnerable*; and all my weapons were broken against me.

But another came unto me saying:

"Behold! I am a *woman-hater*. Not one of them do I trust. Nay, not one can deceive and allure me. For I have *their numbers*, all of them."

And my heart was gladdened. For, by that sign, I knew that he was *easy*. And my way was clear before me.

Verily, verily, men are of three varieties: the kind that must be driven with whip and spur; the kind that must be coaxed with apples and sugar; and the kind that must be blindfolded and *backed* into the shafts of matrimony.

And the woman-hater is like unto the last.

BOOK OF FLIRTS

Therefore, I charge thee, when thou meetest one of these seek not to argue with him, neither to convince him; but *agree* with him sweetly, that all thy sex is weak and untrustworthy.

Discourse sorrowfully upon the *pitfalls* of flirtation, and the *hollowness* of love, and the *horrors* of matrimony.

Declare boldly thy scorn for the New Woman, and for the Old Woman, and for the Frivolous Woman, and for the Highbrow, and for the Lowbrow, and all the women that are on the earth and in the heavens above the earth.

And when thou hast disarmed him, taking all his arguments from out his mouth, speak sweetly concerning the beauties of *platonic friendship* and wax rapturous in its praises.

Bring the cushion for his head, and the footstool for his feet, and feed him from the chafing dish with the fruits of thine own cooking, saying:

"I prithee, *do* smoke, for it is so *chummy!* Yea, I beg of thee, treat me as thou wouldst a *man* friend."

Let him hold thy hand.

[40]

BOOK OF FLIRTS

And he shall say in his heart:

"Would to heaven I were not a Woman Hater, and that all women were like unto her; for she is *sensible* and *sincere* – and a bachelor flat was never like *this!*"

And upon the seventh evening he shall fall down before thee and retract all his words, eating them one by one.

And when thou remindest him of thy warnings and of thy fear of marriage, he will seek to persuade thee and will comfort thee with kisses and a solitaire.

Then shalt thou slip the bridle over his head and the reins shall be in *thine* hands. And there shall be *one less* Woman Hater in the world.

For a *Woman Hater*, my Beloved, is like unto the simple ostrich, which hideth its head in the sand and thinketh itself safe.

But he that professeth open adoration is like unto the park squirrel, which will eat out of thine hand but can *never be caught!*

[41]

BOOK OF FLIRTS

Chapter Six

MY Daughter, a woman is a study in moods and tenses, but man is a simple proposition which worketh according to a "system."

Behold, how the two regard a letter. For when a woman writeth she spelleth her soul out on paper; but a man putteth all his *tender* meanings between the lines. Yea, a woman's letter is a confession, but a man's letter is a veiled allusion which *concealeth* his thoughts. Verily, it is a work of *art*.

Yet, when a woman receiveth it, she readeth it over many times, and placeth it within her shirtwaist by day, and under her pillow by night. For she knoweth that, with temptations like unto telephones and post-cards within reach, a *hand-written letter* is a sign of devotion.

But, when a man receiveth a woman's letter, he droppeth it in his pocket. Nay, not in the pocket above his heart, but in that pocket which containeth the fewest bills and receipts and lead pencils and other *valuable* things.

He carryeth it there faithfully – until he changeth his coat.

He layeth it away in an unused drawer amongst other trash.

He forgetteth it.

And, when years shall have passed, he findeth it and taketh it out curiously.

He regardeth it with astonishment.

He wrinkleth his brows with his great effort at recollection, saying: "Now who the dickens wrote this thing? Yea, *who* is 'Mabel'?"

He giveth it up.

And lo! he proceedeth to make pipe-lighters of thine heart-to-heart effusion.

Behold thy letter, like unto his love, goeth up in smoke!

SELAH!

Few Thy Rings, but
Many Thy Bangles;
for a Musical Jingle
Fascinateth Him, even
as the Sound of a Rattle
Fascinateth a Babe.

BOOK OF DAMSELS

Chapter One

GIVE ear, my Daughter, and receive my wisdom, for the *husband-hunt* leadeth over many hurdles and the trail of the Eligible Thing aboundeth in pitfalls.

Lo, the woods are full of men, but men are full of strange suspicions; and in elusiveness the fox is simple beside them.

I charge thee, seek not to be a fashion-plate; for a human "shriek" giveth warning and affrighteth the game. Verily a *becoming* frock of home manufacture is more to be desired than a French creation which maketh thee to resemble a bad dream!

Costly thy smile as thy dentist shall make it; for a pearl in the mouth exceedeth two on the finger. And it is better to be dead than *unkissable*.

Cheap thy gloves, if need be, but expensive thy sachet; for a man knoweth not scent from sentiment.

Few thy rings, but many thy bangles; for a musical jingle fascinateth him even as the sound of a rattle fascinateth a babe. Yea, manicured nails and

[47]

perfectly clean cuffs are more to be desired in the world of business than a knowledge of stenography.

Modest thy hats, yet chic withal; and thy hair glorious. For a *cheap coiffure* is an abomination, but a made-to-order switch is a woman's "crown of beauty."

Look not upon the rouge-pot when it is too red, but delicate thy blushes and thy complexion put on with a fine brush and self-restraint.

Plain thy coat, but frilly thy petticoat and of all silk; for a feminine "swish" is as poetry unto the masculine ear.

Then, I say unto thee, waste not thy substance upon style. For a man knoweth not last year's left-over from this year's fad, but he knoweth a "vision" when he seeth her.

Verily, a wise virgin hideth her light under a bushel of simplicity, but a foolish damsel goeth forth resembling a human snare. She painteth her cheek as with house paint, and gildeth her hair with much gold. She adorneth herself with feathers and weareth dangling ear-rings. And at sight of her men fly on wings of fear.

[48]

BOOK OF DAMSELS

Chapter Two

HEAR now, the Prayer of a Damsel of Babylon, which she chanteth in her heart: Angels and Ministers of Grace, oh, hear me! Bestow upon me, I pray thee:

The smile of a seraph.

The voice of a dove.

The silence of the Sphinx.

The eyes of an houri.

The blindness of a bat.

The figure of a cloak model.

The wisdom of Solomon.

The ways of a kitten.

The conscience of a cat.

The self-control of a tin soldier.

The pliability of a sofa cushion.

The capriciousness of an automobile.

The sensitiveness of a suet pudding.

The intelligence of a pet clam.

[49]

BOOK OF DAMSELS

The sweetness of a cream puff.

The ambition of a potato.

The meekness of a door-mat.

The opinions of an echo.

The fascinations of a chorus girl.

The patience of Griselda.

The mystery of the Catacombs.

The faith of a poodle.

And the endurance of Atlas.

These things I ask in order that I may be *all* things unto *one* man!

BOOK OF DAMSELS

Chapter Three

H OW little, O, my Daughter, how exceeding little shall satisfy the heart of a woman!

For a man's love is like unto an orchid, which requireth tender persuasion and *constant cultivation*. But a woman's love is like unto an air plant, which flourisheth continually upon *imagination*.

Now, I knew a damsel of Babylon, and she was exceeding fair, having dove's eyes, and curling locks, and much moneys, and a motor car.

Wherefore the youths of the land flocked unto her house, and her parlor was always *full*, and her piazza running over.

And one of these was a medal-winner, called Clod, who possessed a football figure and a Gibson profile. But the least among them all was Wisenheimer, who was abbreviated and whose hair was thin upon the top.

And Clod come unto the damsel, bringing his medals and his loving cups and divers trophies. And when he had shown them all and had told her of his deeds

[51]

of prowess, he sat afar off in a corner and conversed of *generalities* and of *himself*.

For he said in his heart, "When she hath seen what great works I am destined to accomplish, then will she gladly share them with me and shine in my reflected glory."

But Wisenheimer concentrated all his conversation upon *one topic*, saying:

"How marvellous are thine eyes to-night, O Star of Beauty! And thy lips have a curve like unto the smile of Mona Lisa. Thy hair is of a wonderful softness; and *what* is that fascinating perfume thou usest? Lo, many damsels have I known, but thou excellest them all; for thou art as Maxine Elliot and Lillian Russell and the Venus de Milo in one!"

And the damsel was interested, and she said:

"Go on!"

Then Wisenheimer cast himself before her crying: "Lo, what am I, a worm and a parasite, that I should aspire to thy love?

"Behold, I am a *sinner* and full of *evil*, yet I need the love of a *noble woman* to save me! I am as *nothing*, and have accomplished nothing, yet I yearn for the inspiration of an angel to guide me and sustain me and spur me on to higher things!"

And lo, the maiden fell upon his neck and comforted him with kisses and with promises. And the wedding was set for October.

Yet all her friends said:

"What doth she see in *him!*"

But I say unto thee, the maiden was wise. For verily, verily, in the comedy of matrimony there is more joy in being a *star* than in being an *understudy!*

BOOK OF DAMSELS

Chapter Four

BEHOLD, my Daughter, how Man's taste concerning women hath changed!

For lo, it hath come to pass that a maiden of sweet and simple sixteen is, unto a matron of fair and frivolous forty, as breakfast food unto caviar and old wine.

Yea, a man no longer yearneth for a babe to cuddle; and a clinging vine fretteth him, as a shoe that squeaketh or a chair that wobbleth. Moreover, he desireth *rich* things. And a widow with many shekels hath a more solid attraction than a damsel with naught but beauties of the soul.

Go to! The kiss of a damsel of sixteen is more insipid than pink ice-cream, but the kiss of a woman of forty hath the flavor of experience and vera violetta.

Lo, a damsel worshippeth a man as a demi-god and discourseth unto him of her "ideals"; but a matron *mothereth* him and cooeth unto him in *baby talk*. A damsel discusseth the *weather* with a youth and singeth "The Rosary" unto him; but a woman of

BOOK OF DAMSELS

forty discusseth *his talents* and singeth him lullabies. A maiden babbleth on as the brook, thinking to be *always* amusing, but a matron knoweth that after his labors of the day a man preferreth a down pillow unto fireworks.

A maiden pouteth and chafeth beneath his "moods," but a matron ascertaineth whether they proceed from indigestion or an ingrowing temperament, and healeth them accordingly with soda mints or flattery.

A maiden seeketh to appear *mysterious*, and romantic, but a matron playeth always the *platonic friend*. She is *so* simple.

A maiden goeth roundabout ways to hasten a proposal, but a matron *seemeth to put it off*. She forbiddeth him to speak of marriage, even as she forbiddeth a small boy to touch the medicine which she hath determined he shall swallow. And lo, he yearneth straightway therefor.

Verily, verily, a maiden goeth forth with the sound of bugles and an airgun, but a matron setteth her trap in unseen places and lieth low.

[55]

BOOK OF DAMSELS

A maiden *challengeth* a man with coquettishness, but a matron putteth him to *sleep!* For no man goeth into matrimony with his eyes open! Verily, verily, he falleth in love as he falleth out of bed, and awakeneth with a great shock, knowing not *how it hath happened.*

BOOK OF DAMSELS

Chapter Five

HAST thou heard the tale of the wise and foolish virgins, oh, my Daughter? Then hearken! For this parable pointeth a great moral.

Now, the foolish virgin cried unto her sisters, early in the season, "Lo! the spirit of the love-chase is upon me! I must be up and doing. For the summer resort shall be my happy hunting ground, where the game is easy and plentiful."

And she went her ways rejoicing, armed with three trunks and a pink parasol and girded about with lingerie frocks and a silk bathing suit.

Yet, when she had arrived upon the scene, behold there was naught within sight! Lo, each morning she wandered upon the beach with one callow college-youth and each evening danced gladly with a flirtatious octogenarian. All the damsels of the hotel, they waltzed in pairs and *pretended* to like it!

But the wise virgin sighed, "Alas! I cannot *afford* to go upon a vacation trip. Nay I must stay in town! For I shall be *busy*."

And she *was* busy!

BOOK OF DAMSELS

For, when all the other women had departed, the men of the town, being much bored and having naught else to do, flocked unto her door and made themselves comfortable upon her piazza.

Yea, in twos and threes came they, the simple youth with his mandolin and the wise youth with his Rubaiyat, the married man in his loneliness, and the bachelor whose sweetheart was abroad.

And she fed them iced drinks and flattery, and they absorbed all of it gladly—and were consoled!

And lo, before the summer had waned she wore six engagement rings; for the harvest was plentiful.

Verily, verily, a summer resort is a place wherein a woman will resort to anything, from a babe unto a grandfather, for amusement; but a womanless town is a ripe field.

BOOK OF DAMSELS

Chapter Six

OH, ye damsels of Babylon! Ye followers after fads and wearers of pearl earrings! How long will ye seek to appear *sophisticated*? How long will ye continue to pose as *cynics*, and think it chic to be satirical and piquant to be capricious?

Know ye not, oh foolish ones, that a man dreadeth a female cynic as a small boy dreadeth an education? Yea, and a satirical damsel is unto him as a caterpillar upon the neck, which maketh him to shudder. But a capricious woman is as gravel in the shoes. She giveth him great *pain*.

Behold, a foolish damsel seeketh always to scintillate. She appeareth clothed in worldly wisdom and bristling with opinions. She provoketh arguments and answereth with repartee. She mocketh at a man's sentiments and rebuketh him with epigrams. She maketh him to look *foolish*.

But a wise damsel is sweeter than distilled honey and more simple than the plot of a Robert Chambers novel. She lighteth her own way with the sun of her smiles, and smootheth all her paths with soft soap. She seeketh not her own glorification but poureth oil upon the vanity of the just and unjust alike.

Doth a youth argue with her, she is easily convinced and covereth him with approbation, saying: "How didst thou *ever* think of *that*?"

And, lo, his argument is broken against him.

Doth her Beloved call at eve, bringing with him the *grouch* "that knoweth no brother", she greeteth him with the *smile* that knoweth no sister.

She ministereth unto him with cooling drinks and looks of sympathy.

She bringeth him the ash-tray and the shaded lamp and the foot-stool and the newspapers.

She urgeth him to *smoke*.

She forbeareth to *talk*.

And behold his mood dissolveth as the mist before the sun, and he exclaimeth in his heart: "Good Heavens! What would life *be* without this *woman!*"

He proposeth.

[60]

BOOK OF DAMSELS

And all the days of her life she treadeth upon velvet.

Verily, verily, a wise woman preferreth peace of mind unto her own opinions, *comfort* unto her dignity, and an *husband* unto a reputation for brilliancy. She saith in her heart:

"I am not here to *reform* him, but to *please* him."

And, lo, all the world is her *roller coaster!* For the price of *peace* is a *perpetual smile!*

SELAH.

Verily, Verily, My Daughter, the Fool Hath Said in Her Heart, "All Men Should Marry! For There is a Reason for Everything Under the Sun, Save a Bachelor"

BOOK OF BACHELORS

Chapter One

GO to, my Daughter. Knowest thou a man who hat lived long in a bachelor flat? Then beware of him! For his ways are full of guile and he hath not a thrill left.

Alas, the bachelor flat is a curse sent upon Woman. For, lo, though a man hath dwelt in the back hallroom of a boarding-house for many years and hath suffered all its untold horrors, the moment he taketh a flat the sweet feminine thing seeketh him out and yearneth to make him "comfortable."

And his days are made sad with sofa pillows and towel racks, and picture frames, and shaving pads, and foot-stools, until his house resembleth a bargain counter, or the spoils from the harem of a sacked city.

He groaneth when he seeketh in corners for a spot wherein to place his forty-seventh cushion; he curseth when he returneth after dark and falleth over tabourets and *other* evidences of the *pursuit of man*; he laugheth as he borroweth old socks from his men friends that he may supply *all* of those who desire to do his mending. And to him, in matters of love, there is nothing new under the sun.

For the man that weddeth a widow is number two, but the woman that weddeth a bachelor-flatee is number *forty-two*.

And when she mendeth his coat and patteth his pillow; when she kisseth him in the cleft within his chin and runneth her fingers through his hair, he feeleth no thrill. For these are unto him but as a tale that hath been many times told.

Verily, his sentiments are frayed at the edges and his emotions worn thin with usage. His heart is patched in many places and his illusions are as last year's roses – withered.

Yea, his love is but as warmed-over pudding or cold veal served upon the second day; even as second-hand furniture, whereof the interior is motheaten.

But he is better than *nothing*.

BOOK OF BACHELORS

Chapter Two

VERILY, verily, my Daughter, the fool hath said in her heart, "All men should marry! For there is a reason for everything under the sun, save a *bachelor*."

But I have gone among the bachelors, questioning them, young and old; and I say unto thee, the "*reasons*" why a man taketh a *stimulant* are not more numerous and wonderful than the reasons why he doth not marry.

Behold, he doth not marry:

Because he is too *young*.

Because he is too *old*.

Because he hath not *thought* about it.

Because he hath thought *too much* about it.

Because he is poor and cannot *afford* a wife.

Because he is rich and doth not *require* a wife.

Because he loveth *no* woman,

Because he loveth *all* women.

Because he hath not met the *right* woman.

[67]

BOOK OF BACHELORS

Because he *hath* met the right woman and been "disappointed."

Because he hath many *illusions* concerning women.

Because he hath *no* illusions concerning them.

Because *no* woman is good enough.

Because *he* is not "good enough" for *any* woman.

Because he is not ready to *settle down*.

Because he is *already* settled down, and is content.

Because he is *weak* and fearful.

Because he is *strong* and impregnable.

And, likewise –just *because*.

[68]

BOOK OF BACHELORS

Chapter Three

HEARKEN, my Daughter, unto the parable of the merrie bachelor; hearken and be comforted.

For, I say unto thee, not one of these liveth but shall receive his just desert!

Now, in my youth, there came unto me such an one, saying, "*Why* shall I marry? For lo, have I not *all* the comforts of home, at *half* the expense? Behold, I have three good meals a day and a den filled with gew-gaws, which are the work of many damsels. Yea, and not one of them but yearneth to sew on my buttons.

"Moreover, I can go forth into the country in the summer time without having to pawn mine overcoat; and in the winter I can go unto my club without having to perjure my soul.

"Verily, verily, my life is like unto an eleven-course dinner.

"For on Monday I may talk art unto a high-browed damsel; and on Tuesday I may talk *love* unto a widow; and on Wednesday I may talk *nonsense* unto a fluffy thing.

BOOK OF BACHELORS

"But a married man must talk *domestic economy* unto the *same woman* every night, which is like a table d'hote menu, of a deadening monotony.

"Behold, I offer no apology for my singleness; for I am *unashamed!* And my one fear is that I shall awaken from this *dream!*"

And I answered him, saying, "Even so!" Yet, as time passed, the hairs dropped one by one from the head of the bachelor, until it shone as a great light.

Lo, from eating and drinking much good food and having no *worries*, he became round and pudgy, like unto a Billiken.

And the maidens of the land who had trembled at his approach now tittered merrily at sight of him. Yea, whereas, before, he had been able to spend an whole evening with one of them, bringing a box of cheap candy, he now spent all his savings upon them.

For it requireth real orchids and champagne to make a fat man *fascinating*.

And he observed the married men of his acquaintance, that from overworking they had still kept their figures and were *interesting*. Yea, and they flirted with their stenographers and were merry; but the bachelor not having to labor had accomplished nothing; for he had spent his days in yawning.

Then he came unto me, crying:

"Lo! At last I would marry and settle down. But she that I once loved hath married another. And how shall I choose a wife? For all women are as *one* woman unto me."

And I mocked him with my ha-has, saying:

"My Son, I adjure thee, wed any woman thou *canst!* For the buds of the Nation are *not* collecting antiques. Yet, peradventure, one of these shall accept thee as a *good thing*; or another shall take thee as a *last resort*, when she hath passed her fifth season. Go to! Thou hast eaten the bread of life without *honey* thereon, and thou shalt hereafter be satisfied with the *crumbs*."

Verily, verily, life without love is as a pipe without a light; but a man without a wife is as a helpless barge without a tow-boat.

BOOK OF BACHELORS

Chapter Four

MY Daughter, hear now the Thanksgiving Day prayer of a bachelor:

Oh, Lord, I thank Thee that Thou hast vouchsafed me another year of *freedom*. That I am still safe!

That Thou hast made me what I *am* – wise, unconquerable, immune!

That, although I have many times lost my heart, I have never yet lost my *head*.

That I did not marry my first love.

That, though the hairs of my head be numbered, they are still sufficient to cover my bald spot.

That, though my forehead gradually becometh more *intellectual*, it is not yet bare.

That I have never yet written a letter which could be held against me in a breach-of-promise suit, but have confined all my *tender* messages unto telegrams and postcards.

That all my words have been discreet and mine actions cautious and self-restrained.

BOOK OF BACHELORS

That, although maidens may bestow upon me purple neckties, spotted scarfs, plaid mufflers and orange-colored gloves at Christmastide, I shall not be required to *wear* them.

That I am still regarded as *eligible* among maidens and matrons. That they have not *found me out!*

That, day by day, my heart is acquiring a coat of cement and my conscience a coat of mail.

That I have carefully preserved all my emotions in alcohol!

That there is no marrying nor giving in marriage in Heaven!

Yea, for good cigars, bachelor flats, vaudeville, briar pipes, clubs, apartment hotels, stenographers, comic operas, taxicabs and *widows*, Good Lord I thank Thee!

And now in the name of peace and contentment, vouchsafe me another year of single blessedness.

Yea, give me liberty or give me death! Amen!

SELAH

[73]

When Her Shoe Cometh Untied, When Her Side-Comb Falleth Out, When Her Hair Tumbleth Down, Turn Away Thine Eyes, Lest Thou Be Undone. For Circe was as Naught Beside a Woman with Flowing Hair.

BOOK OF SIRENS

Chapter One

B EHOLD, my Daughter, I have parted from mine Appendix and my conscience is clear! Therefore do I fear but three things in all the world:

And the first of these is a mouse.

And the second is embonpoint.

But the third is a *Trained Nurse*!

For I have watched her at her *work*.

And, I charge thee, in the flutter of her apron there lurketh more danger than in the whole chorus of a comic opera. For a chorus girl practiseth her wiles upon strong men, but *she* seeketh him only that is stricken and at her mercy.

Yea, when he is down-and-out she getteth in her fine work.

Upon her head she weareth a cute cap, which glorifieth her as a halo in his sight. She walketh upon heels of velvet and cooeth unto him in a voice of silver.

[77]

BOOK OF SIRENS

Her smile runneth over and will *not* come off.

She hath dove's eyes.

She batheth his brow with spikenard and myrrh, and anointeth him with alcohol. She arrangeth his pillows and comforteth his soul with words of cheer. *She taketh his pulse!*

He yearneth to be babied – and she babyeth him.

He pineth for sympathy – and she sympathizeth.

He seeketh comfort – and she maketh him *comfortable*.

And what chance hath a damsel at a pink tea beside a ministering angel such as one of these?

Go to, thou Simple One! What strength is there in a *sick* man that he shall flee before all the temptations of St. Anthony, in one?

Nay, though he be of stone and of adamant, though his heart be encased in barbed wire, yet shall he turn upon his pillow sighing:

BOOK OF SIRENS

"Alas Miriam is all right; but a wife was never like this!"

Yet how guileless is human nature! For, ye will keep your silver in a strong box and your jewels behind bars of iron; yet will ye trust your beloved in the hands of one of these.

Verily, verily, the Lorelei is passeé and witches are no more.

But a Little Trained Nurse is a *dangerous thing!*

BOOK OF SIRENS

Chapter Two

VERILY, my Daughter, there be these three: the maid, the matron, and the widow; and the luckiest of these is the *widow*.

For she hath graduated from the School of Experience and her crepe veil glorifieth her as a diploma.

And, though she may live in a bachelor flat, none shall gossip about her; but whatsoever she doeth shall seem "cute" in the eyes of men.

When she talketh wittily they shall not say, "She knoweth too much"; and when she talketh foolishly they shall declare that she but seeketh to *appear* simple. If she smoketh a cigarette, she will make excuse, saying, "Mine *husband* taught me how to do this thing", and all men shall call her "fascinating".

Yea, she possesseth all the glory of matrimony, even unto "Mrs." on her name, and none of the discomforts. She shall marry a second time if she so desireth; and if she doth *not*, who shall say that she *could* not?

BOOK OF SIRENS

For one man hath set his seal of approval upon her, and where one hath led the rest shall follow like unto a flock of Geese. Yea, in the matter of women, man hath great faith in the judgment of his brother, but he doubteth his own taste.

And, though a widow be neither wealthy, nor good to look upon; though she be fat and forty and frivolous; yet she understandeth how to make a man comfortable—which is the secret of all wisdom. She shall feed the lambs from the chafing-dish and the lions with honeyed words; she shall coax the smoker to smoke; she shall hold a match to his cigar; she shall bring a footstool for his feet and a couch pillow for his head; she shall mend his gloves and listen eagerly to his stories unto seven times seven times.

Yet envy her not, my daughter, for hath she not been married once? And a woman who hath once *been married* hath earned whatsoever she receiveth.

BOOK OF SIRENS

Chapter Three

HEED my instructions, oh my Son, that thou mayest understand the Seven Poses of Woman!

For, whether she dwelleth in the high places or in the low places, her nets are cast into the sea, and her hooks are bated with perfume and chafing-dishes and domesticity.

Yea, though she hideth in a studio apartment and cryeth "I shall never marry!", yet doth she seek to lure thee with joss sticks and pink tea and rarebits and the *artistic temperament*.

Likewise, beware when she patteth thy coat lapel; when she slippeth her hand confidingly into thine overcoat pocket be not persuaded. For the touch of a damsel's fingers is alluring, but a *wife's* "touch" is expensive.

Lo, when she mothereth thee; when she runneth her fingers through thy top hair; when she inquireth concerning thy health and urgeth thee to wear rubbers be prepared to escape her; for, so doth she shear the lamb for the slaughter.

When her shoe cometh untied, when her side-comb falleth out, when her hair tumbleth down, in the game of tennis, turn away thine eyes, lest thou be undone. For, Circe was as naught, beside a woman with flowing hair.

When she "turneth" her ankle upon the golf links, I charge thee do not bear her in thine arms to safety; but, for thy soul's sake, flee in search of a doctor, 'ere she turneth thine head also.

When she putteth perfume upon thy locks, oh beware of her! For she doeth this that she may mark thee for *her own*; and, until it be washed away, thou shalt be covered with shame in the eyes of the world.

But, when she coaxeth thee to be adorned, when she seeketh to *manicure thy nails*; when she patteth thy fingers and yearneth to bathe them with sweet ointments; when she weareth a cute apron and sitteth more near, I charge thee, clasp thine hands behind thee, crying:

[83]

"Nay! Thou mayest *hold* them, but thou shalt *not manicure* them!"

For by this strategy fell the Benedicts.

Go to, my Son! Ask me not how I have learned of Woman, concerning all her *poses*.

For lo, I am a *woman*, and I have *tried* them.

[84]

BOOK OF SIRENS

Chapter Four

THE secret musings of thy Father Solomon, found in his diary, concealed in the pocket of his smoking jacket and privily copied by thy Mother.

Read now his libellous words, my Daughter, and ponder thereon; for he hath known much girt:

"Verily, verily, in all the world, there be but two things which have power to disconcert me.

"A Meerschaum Pipe is one of these.

"The other is a woman.

"And, so like is the first unto the second, that I doubt not the former is but a reincarnation of the latter.

"Lo, I have colored upward of twenty meerschaums, and have made love unto upward of seven hundred damsels. And I say unto thee, not one of them hath been worth the struggle nor repaid the toil and travail.

"Behold, how a man puchaseth a meerschaum at great price.

[85]

BOOK OF SIRENS

"Behold, how he wooeth a woman at great expense.

"How joyfully he flingeth away his shekels that they may be covered with silver and fine gold!

"How tenderly he encaseth them in velvet!

"With what care and delicacy he wasteth his golden hours in the coloring of his pipe!

"With what pains and ingenuity he wasteth golden years in winning the heart of a woman!

"How lovingly he burneth tobacco for the one!

"How patiently he burneth incense before the other!

"Yet, lo, a sudden coldness – and the pipe hath snapped! A sudden chilliness – and the woman's love is shattered!

"Or let the fire within the meerschaum's bowl wax too hot, or the ardor of his devotion unto the woman wax too intense – and behold the pipe is ruined and the woman is spoiled forever!

"And it is all up with him!

BOOK OF SIRENS

"The fool hath said in his heart, 'All women are as trolley cars, which having once been caught, need no longer be pursued.' But I say unto thee, thy pursuing is never finished; thy task is never done!

"For, seven times seven weeks, mayest thou devote thyself unto a meerschaum, and seven times seven months, unto a damsel!

"Yet if thou layest them aside, and thinkest to cease from thy devotions for but a little while, lo, the pipe hath faded – and the woman hath forgotten thee.

"Verily, verily, there is no rest for a peaceful man! For, life with a pipe, or a woman, is all toil and travail and vexation.

"Yet life *without* them is all weariness and desolation!"

SELAH.

[87]

Verily, Verily, Even Thy Father Solomon Himself, had not More than Enough Wives, for Every Man Requireth at Least Two Soulmates. One to Amuse Him – and One to Wait Upon Him.

BOOK OF ADMONITIONS

Chapter One

MY Daughter, hearken unto my words, and attend diligently to my counsel; for the understanding of *Man* is the beginning of a good income, and a knowledge of *his ways* more profitable than a higher education.

Behold, a woman delighteth to travel the path of love slowly and through devious by-ways of flirtation and sentiment, but a man *rusheth* over it at the speed limit.

Unto a woman, the first kiss is but the *start* in the love chase, but unto a man it is ofttimes the *finish*.

Lo, when a woman weddeth a man, it is in order that she may get him; but when a man weddeth a woman, it is in order that he may prevent *another* from getting her.

Yea, verily, when a woman clingeth unto single blessedness, it is because she hath met *no* man with whom she could endure to live; but, when a man remaineth a bachelor, it is because he hath met no woman *without* whom he *cannot* live.

BOOK OF ADMONITIONS

A man weddeth a woman in order to escape loneliness, and immediately thereafter joineth a *club* in order to escape the woman.

He marryeth a damsel because she appealeth to his "higher nature", and spendeth all the rest of his days seeking after those who appeal to his lower nature.

A woman is cast down with doubts lest a man doth not love her; but a man never troubleth his soul, as to whether or not a woman loveth him, but as to whether or not he *wanteth* her to love him.

Behold, an *honest* woman may cheat at cards, but never at love; but he considereth himself an "*honorable man*" that never cheateth at a game of poker though he never playeth fair at the game of hearts.

Go to! Think no man *in love* while he flattereth thee and extolleth all thy ways; but, when he beginneth to *moralize* and to criticise thy *hats*, then mayest thou plan thy trousseau.

When he saveth thy life it may be for chivalry's sake; but when he carryeth an *umbrella* to please thee it is for love's sake.

[92]

BOOK OF ADMONITIONS

Be not set up when a man giveth thee the key to his heart, for, peradventure, upon the following day, he may *change the lock!*

Then, how shall a woman understand a man, since they are *all* cut upon the *bias!*

Verily, verily, by turning him around, my Daughter, and reading him *backward*, even as a Chinese laundry ticket!

BOOK OF ADMONITIONS

Chapter Two

HOW long, oh, ye Easy Ones, shall men continue to call ye *"kitten"* when they are sentimental and *"cat"* when they wax cynical?

Verily, verily, I say unto thee, the ways of a man are the ways of Grimalkin; for doth not a cat, and likewise a man, prize his *dignity* above all things else in the heavens above, or in the earth beneath, or in the subways under the earth?

Moreover, doth not a cat, and likewise a man, seek out all the *soft* places upon the face of the earth, and all the most *comfortable* spots within the house, and all the *easy* chairs of the office?

Yea, doth not a man, even as a cat, wander abroad at night and return only at mealtimes?

Doth not a cat, and also a man, cling unto the woman that maketh him most *comfortable* and stroketh him the *right* way, but revile and despise her that disturbeth his meditations and arouseth him from his slumbers?

BOOK OF ADMONITIONS

Doth not a cat flee in terror from one that flingeth cold water upon his coat, and a man from her that flingeth cold water upon his vanity?

Doth not a man, like unto a cat, struggle to escape when he is held *tightly*, yet remain cheerfully where he is not wanted?

Doth not a cat, and likewise a man, flee fearfully from that which is flung at his head – whether it be a bone, or a plate, or a *woman*?

And, being "dropped," doth not a cat and likewise a man, land always upon his *feet* and depart in search of consolation?

Lo, if thou pursuest a cat and a man with thine endearments will they not shrink from thee, with vexation ?

But, if thou ignorest them, will they not sit devotedly at thy feet?

Go to ! I say unto thee a *woman* is not as a tabby, but as a Faithful Fido which cannot be shaken off.

[95]

BOOK OF ADMONITIONS

She followeth a man whithersoever he goeth, accepting gladly a pat upon the head and a kind word, and lying down at his feet to be *stepped on.*

Verily, verily, why doth a spinster console herself with a *cat* in her loneliness?

Even because this is the only thing which can be found to resemble a *man*!

BOOK OF ADMONITIONS

Chapter Three

LO, while a man courteth a maiden he saith unto her :

"Beloved, *I adore* the waves and frivols of thy hair! The neatness of thy waistline is my delight ; and what *is* that subtle sachet which maketh thee to remind me always of the rose of morning?"

But in his heart he saith :

"Yet, when we are married, then shall *I teach* her not to wear false ringlets, and the imported complexion which she now putteth on shall she abjure.

"Verily from the using of that *awful scent* shall I break her, and from the wearing of corsets shall I rescue her ! For we shall then be *one*, and I shall be *that one!*"

And while a damsel seeketh to allure a man she saith unto him:

"Thou art *so* sensible. Yea, I pray thee, continue to wear a *comfortable* collar always; for why shalt thou suffer for style's sake? Lo, thy beard and thy mustache, they are so *characteristic*; and in a soft hat thou hast *real personality!*"

BOOK OF ADMONITIONS

But in her heart she muttereth :

"Go to! When I have him *safe*, then shall I entice him to put on a high collar, even unto *four inches*; and the shaving of his face will require but two weeks ! Yea, and that quaint top-piece shall he exchange for a derby within the first month. For I know *just* what he needeth!"

Verily, verily, even in the hour of their courtship, do they prepare for *war!*

Even while she poureth his wine, doth she determine that he shall become a teetotaler ! Even while he passeth her the sweetmeats doth he plan to put her on a *diet*, 'ere she acquire embonpoint.

As enemies before the battle, do they exchange civilities, saying *"How congenial we are!"*

For every woman thinketh to make a man over after a *pattern*, and every man thinketh to remodel a woman according to a *stock* ideal.

Yea, after the honeymoon *each* seeketh to trim the other down and to add all the *modern improvements*.

Then give them the fruit of their labors, which is a *mutual* shock !

BOOK OF ADMONITIONS

Chapter Four

MY Daughter, she that heedeth my instructions shall find a man easier to play upon than a player piano.

Behold, she hath but to press the right key, and he shall repeat all his repertoire, even unto the *confession* of his sins.

Yea, verily, a man rejoiceth in confessions; and nothing delighteth his soul so much as to *repent*. For, then can he return unto his follies with a clear conscience and renewed enthusiasm.

Go to ! *Who* is so virtuous as an husband that hath but *just* received a cold bath and his wife's forgiveness?

Lo, he goeth forth feeling like unto an uncrowned saint.

He is puffed up with *righteousness*.

Yet, before the night cometh, peradventure, he shall again have wobbled from the straight and narrow way.

BOOK OF ADMONITIONS

How long, then, oh my Daughter, shalt thou encourage men to persecute thee with their "I'm so-sorrys", and their "Never-agains"? For, verily, verily, every man believeth that a woman's patience is a thing of India rubber, which will stretch over a multitude of backslidings.

Yea, he hath not a *doubt* that a broken promise may be glued together with kisses, and a broken heart mended with softsoap.

Confessions are but the soothing syrup wherewith he stilleth his conscience. And his sins would lack much joy if he had not the pleasure of "*regretting*" them.

But I say unto thee, a woman's faith is like unto a cobweb which cannot be patched up, once it hath been shattered; and a woman's heart is not as a rubber ball, which reboundeth after it hath been cast down.

Nay, a bride sobbeth "Harold, tell me *all!*"

But after ten years, a wife saith, "Do whatsoever thou pleasest, but come not unto *me* with thy tale of woe. Lo, I am aweary of holding onto Heaven with one hand and onto *thee* with the other. Therefore go thy ways and let me *sleep!*"

Verily, verily, in time, doth a man's penitence *pall* upon a woman; and his kiss of remorse is more to be dreaded than his sins.

For, once love hath cooled, it *may* be warmed-over, yet it is flat and tasteless, even as a Monday luncheon.

BOOK OF ADMONITIONS

Chapter Five

M Y Daughter, observe my counsel, for the heart of a man is like unto a Broadway car, in which there is always room for *one more.*

Behold, in matters of love, a woman is a *specialist*, but a man is a *general practitioner*. Yea, a woman loveth but one *type* – even *one man* – but a man loveth anything which happeneth to be *at hand*.

Lo, he that weddeth a brunette shall ever after seek peroxide blondes; and he that marryeth a pink and yellow *doll* shall acquire a sudden interest in *intellect* and *brunettes*. For *variety* is the spice of love.

Moreover, a woman is an epicure in love, but a man is a gourmand.

In the love-feast, a woman desireth but one course at a time ; but a man relisheth them *all* served *at once*, like unto a dinner at a country inn.

Yea, he mixeth his flirtations, even as he mixeth his libations, and wondereth sadly why he awakeneth always with an headache.

BOOK OF ADMONITIONS

Verily, verily, even thy Father, Solomon, had not more than enough wives. For every man requireth at least two soul-mates.

One for Sundays – and one for week days.

One to amuse him – and one to wait upon him.

One to save his soul – and one to save his pennies.

One to help him make a fortune – and one to help him spend it.

One for his lighter side – and one for his darker side.

One for company, one for comfort, one for inspiration, one for pastime – and many others, for a change.

SELAH.

Lo, My Beloved, Thy Hair is as Stubble and in the Morning It Standeth Aloft as a Shorn Wheat Field. How *Fascinating* Art Thou in Pajamas, When Thy Face is Covered With Shaving Lather!

BOOK OF SONGS

Chapter One

THE Song of a Wife, which is Mrs. Solomon's. Let him praise me with the words of his mouth; for his flattery is sweeter than wine and his kisses are rarer than orchids.

Lo, my Beloved, thy hair is as stubble, and in the morning it standeth aloft, as a shorn wheat field.

Thy cheek is as a Turkish towel, which caresseth mine.

Thy temples are a shining light, which resembleth a silver polish advertisement.

Thou wearest a derby hat. Thy breath is sweet with cloves.

How *fascinating* art thou in pajamas, when thy face is covered with shaving lather!

How beautiful are thy *feet*.

Behold, thou art a collection of habits. Yea, unto these thou art more constant than the *family* cat.

[107]

Whatsoever thou hast done before, *that* shalt thou do forever and in the *same way*.

Thou kissest me once in the morning, once in the evening, and *twice* upon Christmas Day.

Thou clingest unto thine old pipe as unto thy *reputation*. Thou callest every woman by the *same* pet name.

Lo, what would my Beloved be without his habits? Even as a doggie's tail which hath lost its "wag!" But thy *heart*, oh, my Beloved, is full of lightning changes. Its capacity is inexhaustible.

The memory of yesterday's kiss is unto thee as the memory of yesterday's dinner – sweet, but not satisfying.

Yet, though thy heart changeth many times, I, thy wife, am become *one* of thy habits!

Behold thou hast placed "Mrs." upon my name; thou hast glorified me with a wedding ring !

Therefore, I am become thy doormat. Yea, I am as thy footstool.

[108]

BOOK OF SONGS

I shall mend thy socks with rejoicing, and the replacing of thy buttons shall be my delight.

All the days of thy life, shall I clean thy safety razor and put the studs in thy shirts.

Then, cast thine ashes over my dressing table and strew my carpets with cigar stumps.

Let the awnings of mine house be burned and my lace curtains consumed with fire. I shall not murmur.

For I am my Beloved's and there is *naught* else like unto him.

BOOK OF SONGS

Chapter Two

THE Song of Songs, which is the *widow's*.

When I was a *rib*, I spoke as a rib, and all my ways were the ways of a rib.

Lo, I took man *seriously*, even as he took himself. For him did I rush the breakfast – and keep it waiting.

Unto him did I offer up the palm – and the morning paper. All his opinions were right in mine eyes; and because *he* said a thing, it was *so*.

He was the Lord of my Heart, and the Source of mine Income. And in him I saw nothing *funny*; for my sense of humor had not yet been awakened.

He looked at my hats and mocked them. Yet that inverted salad bowl which he called a "derby" did not arouse my mirth. He waxed satirical at the number of my puffs, and my coiffure was a daily target for his wit. Yet, though he cut all the hair from off his head, and left it to grow upon his face, I felt no merriment.

In his conceit, he made of me a human joke.

[110]

BOOK OF SONGS

But now that I am become a widow, I see him as he is. Therefore shall I arise and smite him in his vanity.

Lo, what woman shall take men seriously, once she hath been married unto one of these? For he, that seemeth a thing of beauty and wisdom unto many virgins, is but a child in the eyes of his wife.

She knoweth the source of his opinions; and the padding of his shoulders is not hidden from her. His grouches are always with her and his digestion is her burden.

Go to! I have seen him at his mirror when he worked upon the parting of his hair. He hath borrowed my powder for his chin, and with my perfume hath he anointed himself. My nail-polish and my eau de cologne, they were not safe from him.

I have flattered him and beheld his fall. I have said unto him, "My love, thy judgment is above question and thy common sense above praise !"

And he hath smiled, as one that sippeth a wine of a rare vintage.

BOOK OF SONGS

I have cooed unto him saying:

"Lo, thy reasoning powers and thine acumen are greater than those of Sherlock Holmes !"

And I have observed his secret joy.

I have cried out:

"Oh, *why* didst thou not go upon the stage? For thy shoulders are better than Faversham's and thy profile than E. H. Sothern's!"

And he hath straightway *proposed!*

The youths of the land have I called "Mr. Smith," and the octogenarians addressed as "Silly Boy." The fat man have I called "graceful", and the ourang-outang, "distinguished."

And all of these were overcome.

Their fairy tales have I outstripped with better fairy tales, and their devices with more subtile devices.

Verily, verily, men are as toys in mine hand; and, even as a child, do I delight to play with them.

Lo, she that fisheth for an husband, laboreth against many odds, but she that fisheth for amusement casteth her nets in pleasant waters, and they shall return unto her heavy laden.

BOOK OF SONGS

Chapter Three

THE Litany of the Summer Girl, which she chanteth continuously, morning and night.

Oh, Lord, deliver me from the deadliness of the Summer Resort, and from all the deadly things therein.

From the emptiness of moonlight evenings without a Man, and the hollowness of life without a flirtation, now preserve me.

From the sentimental grafter and the *platonic friend*, oh spare me!

For, the one seeketh after cheap flirtations, and collecteth kisses, as a woman doth trading stamps.

And the other is as a wet powder-rag which sticketh, but availeth nothing. Verily, verily, a breakfast-food without sugar and cream is not more insipid than one of these.

From college youths, which are fresher than spring asparagus and more tender than spring lamb, oh, deliver me!

[113]

BOOK OF SONGS

From old bachelors, which are staler than last year's canned goods, and tougher than cold rarebits, oh, preserve me !

From the hotel "phonograph," which repeateth the same old love-tunes night after night, year in and year out, oh set me free!

From the *impressionist* that cometh down over Sunday, deliver me !

For, when he hath loved me with all his heart, and with all his mind, and with all his impudence, for an whole *week-end*, he shall depart; and the scorners shall delight in their ha-has and the whisperers say, "She was but a temporary distraction!"

From the *summer widower*, that seeketh to return unto flirtation by a by-path, oh, hide me ! For lo, I am not a consolation prize. Neither am I a grafter, coveting other women's troubles.

From all gossip, and freckles, and tan, and sand-in-the-shoes; from the patronizing bride, and the youth that playeth ragtime; from the bathing suit that

[114]

BOOK OF SONGS

shrinketh, and the nose that peeleth; from mosquitoes, and cows and red ants; from hen parties, and springless straw rides, and manless dances, oh, deliver me !

Feed me with bon-bons and stay me with novels!

Lead me beside the full streams, where the fish are plentiful and the fishing worthy of the fishermaiden; that I may, peradventure, find, *one eligible*, who shall rescue me from the Land of Innocuous Desuetude, and usher me into the Kingdom of Matrimony!

BOOK OF SONGS

Chapter Four

THE Song of The Debutante which the Wise Virgin chanteth in her heart:

Oh, Providence in thy mercy, Thee, grant me these three:

A level head, a soft tongue, and a sense of humor! And the greatest of these is a *sense of humor*.

Lo, I do not ask for wealth, neither for beauty, nor for love; for, having a level head, and a soft tongue, all these things shall be added unto me.

I sigh not for the charms of an houri; and curling hair I shall not crave. Yea, though *one* husband be all that is granted unto me in this day of Progressive Matrimony, I shall not murmur.

Though my waist-line increaseth, year by year, and my teeth depart one by one, I shall not be cast down. For, a cheerful disposition shall sustain me, and the smile that cometh not off shall keep me charming.

Though chorus girls marry above me; though I never build mine own bungalow; though my frocks be made over, and my complexion made up, I shall not repine.

[116]

BOOK OF SONGS

For, behold, I shall not take myself *seriously*, neither be filled with false *illusions* concerning men.

Lo, a woman that regardeth herself seriously is a human joke; and a woman that dallyeth with illusions is as a babe that played with matches. She burneth her own fingers.

Though my cooking be deadly, and my shoes "number fives" I shall not despair. For a sense of humor shall cover me as a mackintosh, off which the lemons, that fate casteth at me, shall roll as water. Verily, verily, a woman without a sense of humor is as one that goeth into New Jersey clad in lace hose. She layeth herself bare to constant *stings*; she suffereth untold pangs.

Then grant me, I pray thee, this one panacea:

That I may laugh when men laugh and the point of their jokes shall not escape me.

That I may not tremble at their wrath; neither wither under their sarcasm, nor repine at their grouches.

And that, all the days of my youth, I shall dwell in the enjoyment of life, repartee, and the pursuit of an husband ! Amen.

[117]

BOOK OF SONGS

Chapter Five

INCLINE thine ear, O, my Daughter! For this is the Song of the *Bride*, which containeth all the law and the "profits" of Matrimony.

I thank thee, O, my Beloved; for thou hast chosen me out of the multitude of women that were *after* thee.

Thou hast delivered me from spinsterhood and led me into the House of Bondage.

Thy *brand* is upon me!

I am thy Chattel.

Thy wishes shall be my wishes, thy tastes my tastes, and thy politics my politics.

I shall have no personal opinions before thine and no other thought before *thee*. Only my *tooth brush* shall remain of all mine individuality.

For lo, I have said in my heart, "Couldst thou love this man in a shop-made suit and a polka dot tie? Couldst thou love him though he lost his front hair? Couldst thou love him *without* a collar?"

And my heart hath answered:

"Yea, verily ! For I am the apple of his eye, and he is the source of mine income. Therefore are we truly *mated*."

Then, whatsoever thou doest, my beloved, it shall be right in my sight ; and whatsoever thou wearest thou shalt seem beautiful in mine eyes.

Even in thy *fishing* clothes shall I adore thee; and if thou but concedest to change thy collar and carry one glove when we go forth in public thou shalt appear sufficiently dressy unto *me*.

I shall take great care of thy digestion, and thy devotion will take care of itself. I shall *not* practise my cooking upon thee.

I shall believe whatsoever thou tellest me, even when I know it to be *false*. I shall listen unto thy *fairy tales* with respect.

I shall *delight* in thine imagination and the works thereof.

I shall endeavor to like thee; for love passeth as the whirlwind, but friendship is a rock which endureth forever.

BOOK OF SONGS

I shall not laugh at thee, for I am *sane*.

When thou hookest my frocks crooked I shall not murmur, but shall urge thee on with my cheers and praises. I shall not hear thy mutterings.

I shall remember thy pipe, thy razor, and thy morning newspaper, to keep them holy.

Thy Desk shall be sacred from mine hands. Thou shalt have *one hook* within the closet.

I shall be a *mother* unto thee ; yet shall I permit thee to treat me as a *babe*, that thou mayest rest under thy favorite delusion. Whosoever speaketh against thee I shall rend her with my finger nails and my sarcasm.

I shall learn to be happy *without* thee in order that I may be happy *with* thee, when thou chancest to be at home.

Thou shalt go thy ways untroubled; for I shall not be thy jailer but thy jollier.

Verily, verily, I shall be all things unto thee; even a wife, an angel, a kitten, a cook, a chum, and a siren.

Yea, I shall be thine *whole harem*!

SELAH.

www.ingramcontent.com/pod-product-compliance
Lightning Source LLC
Chambersburg PA
CBHW060945040426
42445CB00011B/1014